Naughty Nathan

I Don't Wanna Wash My Hands

ISBN 979-8-89428-154-4 (paperback)
ISBN 979-8-89526-028-9 (hardcover)
ISBN 979-8-89428-155-1 (digital)

Copyright © 2024 by J. M. Crowe

All rights reserved. No part of this publication may be reproduced, distributed, or transmitted in any form or by any means, including photocopying, recording, or other electronic or mechanical methods without the prior written permission of the publisher. For permission requests, solicit the publisher via the address below.

Christian Faith Publishing
832 Park Avenue
Meadville, PA 16335
www.christianfaithpublishing.com

Printed in the United States of America

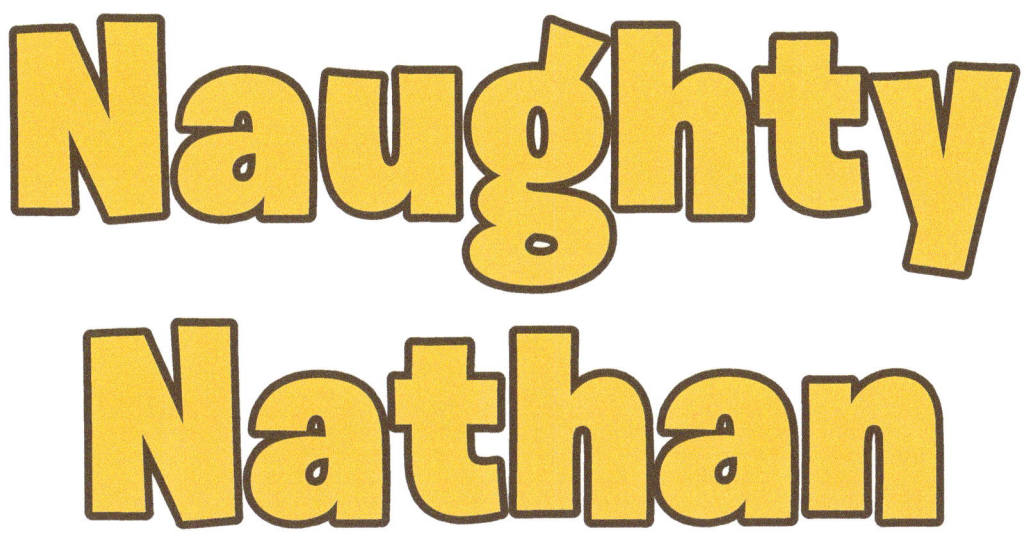

I Don't Wanna Wash My Hands

J. M. Crowe

Nathan loves to play outside, rain or shine. He runs, jumps, crawls, and plays in puddles. His favorite thing to do is to play in the dirt and mud. He digs into the dirt and mud to find bugs.

Nathan uses his fingers to dig through the dirt and mud. Dirt and mud go everywhere. As Nathan throws the dirt and mud, it covers his fingers, fingertips, and fingernails. He has gotten all dirty!

Nathan's mom calls him inside from playing. She has made Nathan a delicious sandwich and cut him some fruit. Nathan comes inside and sits down at his plate. This is his favorite meal. Nathan is covered in mud!

Mom asks Nathan to clean up before eating. Mom tells Nathan to clean his face and wash his hands. He is so dirty!

Nathan tells his mom, "I don't wanna!" Nathan picks up his sandwich with his dirty hands and takes a big bite with mud on his face.

That night, Mom asks Nathan to brush his teeth and get ready for bed. Mom tells Nathan to wash his hands and face before he goes to sleep.

"I don't wanna!" Nathan tells Mom.

Nathan brushes his teeth with his dirty hands and face. Nathan crawls into bed dirty.

Nathan wakes up and goes to school the next day.

"Pee-ew!" says Nathan's classmates. "What is that all over your hands and face?" they ask.

Nathan tells them that he was looking for bugs in the dirt and mud.

Nathan's teacher asks him to wash his hands and face before art class. Nathan says, "I don't wanna!" and begins to pick up the art supplies used by other kids. Nathan paints Mom a picture to take home to be placed on the refrigerator. Nathan gets covered in paint!

Nathan sits down at lunch. Nathan looks at his plate and sees chicken nuggets, fruit, and vegetables. Nathan's teacher tells him to wash his hands and face before eating.

"I don't wanna!" Nathan tells his teacher. He picks up a chicken nugget and takes a big bite.

Once Nathan gets home, he goes outside to play. While outside, Nathan starts to not feel so good. Nathan feels his tummy rumbling. Nathan sits down and holds his belly. Mom comes outside to see how his day was. Nathan tells Mom, "Mom, I don't feel good. My tummy hurts."

Nathan's mom scoops him up and brings Nathan inside. Mom pours a nice warm bath for Nathan to lie in. Nathan crawls into the bath and lies on his back. Mom begins washing his hair and face.

"Mom, why does my tummy hurt?" Nathan asks Mom.

Mom tells Nathan, "During the day, we touch things that have germs on them, things like dirt, mud, and items other people have touched and played with. Those germs get on our hands. We must wash away the germs with warm water and soap before we touch our food or toys."

"Like this, Mom?" asks Nathan. Nathan pours soap in his hands and uses the warm water from the bath to wash his hands.

"That's exactly right!" Mom tells Nathan. "The soap will clean our hands and make them smell good too. Washing our hands will help you not get a tummy ache."

Mom tells Nathan, "Make sure to listen to Mom and your teacher when you are asked to wash your hands. We want you to stay happy and healthy to play in the dirt and mud and to be able to paint awesome pictures!"

The end

About the Author

J. M. Crowe was born and raised and lives in a small suburb outside Atlanta, Georgia. He has a beautiful wife and three small children that he loves dearly. His spare time is spent with family, at the ballpark with the kids, fishing, hunting, and writing.

J. M. began his storytelling at a young age. He loves to talk and meet new people. Once his children were born, J. M. would make up stories to help put his children to bed. Now that his children are older, he writes short stories to help them read. This has turned into a love for writing children's books and building memories with his family.

Printed in the USA
CPSIA information can be obtained
at www.ICGtesting.com
LVHW070827190924
791525LV00003B/78

9 798895 260289